Developing Literacy
TEXT LEVEL
TEXT-LEVEL ACTIVITIES FOR THE LITERACY HOUR

year
3

Ray Barker

Christine Moorcroft

A & C BLACK

Reprinted 2001 (twice), 2002 (twice), 2003, 2004
Published 2000 by
A & C Black Publishers Limited
37 Soho Square, London W1D 3QZ
www.acblack.com

ISBN 0-7136-5318-3

Acknowledgements

The authors and publishers are grateful for permission to reproduce the following:

page 9: extract from *The Bongleweed* by Helen Cresswell, reproduced by permission of Oxford University Press;
page 10: extract from pages 49–51 of *The Twits* by Roald Dahl, published by Jonathan Cape and Penguin Books;
page 12: extract from *A Necklace of Raindrops* copyright © Joan Aiken Enterprises Ltd,
reproduced by permission of A M Heath & Co. Ltd. on behalf of the author;
extract from page 5 of *One Nil* by Tony Bradman (Viking Kestrel, 1987) Copyright © Tony Bradman, 1985,
reproduced by permission of Penguin Books Ltd;
extract from page 7 of *The Hundred-Mile-An-Hour Dog* by Jeremy Strong, published by Penguin;
extract from *Wizziwig and the Weather Machine* by Geraldine McCaughrean, first published in the UK by
Orchard Books in 1995, a division of The Watts Publishing Group Limited, 96 Leonard Street, London EC2A 4XD;
page 17: extract from *The Little Sea Horse* by Helen Cresswell, Text Copyright © 1964 by Helen Rowe,
reproduced by permission of Hodder and Stoughton Limited;
page 20: extract from 'The Snail' © James Reeves from *Complete Poems for Children* (Heinemann),
reprinted by permission of the James Reeves Estate;
page 23: ''Quack!' Said the Billy-goat' from *Collected Poems for Children* by Charles Causley, published by Macmillan;
page 36: extract from *Harry Potter and the Philosopher's Stone* by J K Rowling, published by Bloomsbury Publishing Plc.

Every effort has been made to trace copyright holders and to obtain their permission for use of copyright material.
The authors and publishers would be pleased to rectify in future editions any error or omission.

The authors and publishers would like to thank the following teachers
for their advice in producing this series of books:

Jane Beynon; Hardip Channa; Ann Hart; Lydia Hunt;
Rita Leader; Madeleine Madden; Helen Mason; Kim Pérez;
Joanne Turpin; Fleur Whatley

A CIP catalogue record for this book is
available from the British Library.

Printed in Great Britain by
St Edmundsbury Press Ltd, Bury St Edmunds, Suffolk.

A & C Black uses paper produced with elemental chlorine-free pulp,
harvested from managed, sustainable forests.

Contents

Introduction

Developing Literacy: Text Level supports the teaching of reading and writing by providing a series of activities to develop children's ability to recognise, appreciate and write different genres, styles and purposes of text. In **Year 3** the children compare different story settings; recognise the conventions used in dialogue; investigate the language of stories and poetry; give (and justify) their views about characters; and summarise the main points of stories in the correct sequence. The children develop skills in writing character studies; they learn to plan increasingly longer stories, splitting them into chapters.

The activities in **Year 3** consolidate the children's understanding of the differences between fiction and non-fiction books; they develop their ability to use non-fiction books and learn to use a library classification system. They develop their skills in summarising texts and consolidate their skills in writing alphabetical texts such as glossaries and directories.

The activities are designed to be carried out in the time allocated to independent work during the Literacy Hour. They support the objectives of the National Literacy Strategy *Framework for Teaching* at text level and they incorporate strategies which encourage independent learning – for example, ways in which the children can check their own work or that of a partner. Investigation is given greater emphasis as the series progresses towards **Year 6**.

Year 3 helps children to:
- develop skills in reading and writing fiction and poetry through shared reading and writing;
- be aware of the ways in which story settings are written and to write their own;
- be aware of the different voices in a text and to understand and use the conventions of writing dialogue;
- read, perform and write playscripts;
- identify the themes of stories and poems and compare the ways in which different writers treat them;
- recognise the sequence of events in a story and to plan their own stories using formats which help them to structure the sequence in paragraphs or, for longer stories, in chapters;
- identify and use the features of story language;
- recognise the purposes of the openings and endings of stories and to write effective openings and endings for their own stories;
- write book reviews and character studies;
- use language in order to build up atmosphere or effect;
- distinguish between, and to write, rhyming and non-rhyming poetry;
- appreciate language features of poems, such as alliteration, onomatopoeia, rhyme and rhythm;
- write their own poems and rhymes based on the structures of those they read;
- perform poems and write their own performance poems.

Year 3 also develops the children's ability to:
- read and write non-fiction through shared, guided and independent reading and writing;
- describe the differences between fiction and non-fiction books;
- read, follow, evaluate and write simple instructions;
- identify the purposes of, and to evaluate, different instructional texts;
- be aware of the organisation of, and devices used in, instructions and to use this to write instructions;
- write alphabetical texts;
- select, evaluate and use non-fiction books to find specific information and to answer questions;
- skim and scan texts for a purpose;
- identify the key words and phrases in texts;
- use simple formats on which to express the main points of a text;
- make notes in different ways and to organise their notes;
- write simple recounts and non-chronological reports.

Extension

Most of the activity sheets end with a challenge (**Now try this!**) which reinforces and extends the children's learning and provides the teacher with an opportunity for assessment. These more challenging activities might be appropriate for only a few children; it is not expected that the whole class should complete them. On some pages there is space for the children to complete the extension activities, but others will require a notebook or separate sheet of paper.

Organisation

Few resources are needed besides a computer, scissors, glue, word-banks, readily available general reference material (books and CD-ROMs), information books, leaflets, brochures and a range of dictionaries.

To help teachers to select appropriate learning experiences for their pupils, the activities are grouped into sections within each book. The pages need not be presented in the order in which they appear in the books, unless otherwise stated.

Teachers' notes

Brief notes are provided at the bottom of most pages. They give ideas and suggestions for making the most of the activity sheet, including the use of supplementary materials such as texts and everyday school items. They may make suggestions for the whole class introduction, the plenary session or for follow-up work using an adapted version of the activity.

Structure of the Literacy Hour

The following chart shows an example of the way in which an activity from this book can be used to achieve the required organisation of the Literacy Hour.

Word-play (page 26)

Whole class introduction	**15 min**
Read the poem aloud with the children. Re-read the first line and ask them to explain 'a sheet on a river bed'. Re-read the second line and ask the children which is the word with two meanings ('head'): what are the two meanings?	

Whole class activity	**15 min**
Ask the children to think of words with two meanings. Provide some for them, for example: *face* (human and clock), *ear* (human and corn) and *blade* (grass and knife). Compile a 'two meanings' word-bank to which the children can add as they think of others and to which they can refer for ideas for their poems.	

Group work	**20 min**	**Independent work**	**20 min**
The children could write their own poems based on the structure of **Have you ever seen?** Start them off with 'Have you ever seen eyes on the face of a clock? Or a computer key opening a lock?'		The others work independently from **Word-play** (page 26, **Developing Literacy: Text Level Year 3**).	

Whole class plenary session	**10 min**
The children who have written poems could read them to the others, who could contribute ideas for improving them. Some of those who have completed the activity sheet could read out any new words which they learned and tell the others their meanings.	

Using the activity sheets

Fiction and poetry: reading comprehension

Story settings (page 9) develops the children's appreciation of the ways in which an author can create an image of the story setting so that the reader can 'see' it in his or her mind. Settings are often described visually, but this one lists the aromas of the potting sheds and outhouses in a way which enables the reader almost to smell them. Because there are few adjectives to describe smells, the children (like the author of the passage) can name smells rather than describe them.

In **Voices** (page 10) the children learn to distinguish the different voices (including that of the narrator) in a story.

The Gingerbread Man: a play (page 11) introduces the conventions of playscripts: the way in which dialogue is presented and the use of stage directions.

Story openings (page 12) develops the children's ability to assess what a story is about and the kind of story it is from its opening. They begin by listing the facts revealed by the opening sentences.

Story theme: good and evil (page 13) helps the children to recognise a common theme in traditional stories. They can find the same theme in other texts suggested in the *Framework* for Year 3: myths, legends, parables and adventure stories.

Describing a character (page 14) develops the children's ability to recognise the ways in which an author creates a character. They begin by noting their impressions of the character, Androcles, and then identify the words which gave them this impression.

Penfriend characters (page 15) is designed to be used with any story. The children describe a character's interests, personal qualities and talents and use the information which others have written about story characters to select a character whose penfriend he or she could become.

Story review (page 16) can be used with any story. It provides a format to help the children to record and justify their opinions.

In **Atmosphere** (page 17) the children learn about the ways in which an author can create the atmosphere of a story, chapter or paragraph. They begin by noting their impressions, and then identify the words which gave them this impression.

Stories in the third person (page 18) develops the children's awareness of the person in which a story is written and directs their attention to the words which indicate the person. It links with sentence-level work on the differences between the first and third persons (which focuses on the changes in verbs, nouns and pronouns).

Real life and fiction (page 19) develops the children's appreciation of the differences between real-life and fictional accounts. They should notice the use of interesting verbs, adjectives and adverbs in a fictional account as well as in the description of a character's (possibly the narrator's) thoughts.

The same but different: 1 and **2** (pages 20–21) develop the children's appreciation of the different views presented in poems about the same subject. A structure is provided to help the children to compare the two poems.

Bird words (page 22) develops the children's appreciation of the ways in which language can be used in poetry to create an effect, for example: by using powerful verbs such as 'startles' to suggest the effect of the duck taking off, and the adjective 'flopping' to describe the crows in flight.

In **Perform a poem** and **Performance planner** (pages 23–24) the children read a humorous poem which contains animal noises made by the wrong animals. The children are required to think about the best way in which to perform the poem (taking into account stressed words and lines) and are provided with a structure on which to plan their performance.

Riddles (page 25) develops the children's appreciation of this form of humorous poetry. They have to think hard in order to work out the humour of the poems, which might not be obvious at first. Answers: 1e, 2a, 3d, 4c, 5f and 6b.

Word-play (page 26) develops the children's awareness of the use of double meanings in puns, jokes and humorous poems.

Calligrams (page 27) introduces this type of 'shape poem' in its simplest form: the making of expressive shapes evoked by words. Some children might need more practice in writing single-word calligrams before they attempt the extension activity.

Alliteration (page 28) develops the children's awareness of alliterative sound patterns in poems. They could collect examples of alliteration in poetry and describe the effects which poets create by using alliteration.

Fiction and poetry: writing composition

What did they say? (page 29) provides a wordless picture story: the children add the dialogue, writing in the speech bubbles on the pictures. The pictures contribute to the telling of the story.

In **Script planner** (page 30) the children return to the story with dialogue, which they planned on page 29, and convert it into a playscript. The activity focuses the children's attention upon the ways in which dialogue can be presented (linking with sentence-level work on speech bubbles and speech marks) and requires them to think about the information, other than speech, which they need to provide for the actors and producer of the play.

Collecting ideas for a story (page 31) is a planning sheet, the layout of which helps the children to generate ideas for a story before they begin to plan its structure (opening, main events and so on). This sheet is based on stories in familiar settings and provides a context within which the children can produce ideas for a story. It introduces the use of flow charts to help the children to record their initial ideas for a story before they begin to structure them.

Writing a story opening (page 32) provides a framework to help the children to plan the opening of a story on a familiar setting and theme. They could first brainstorm about the title 'New neighbours' and record their ideas on a flow chart.

Writing a story ending (page 33) provides a structure to help the children to plan the ending of a story. It helps them to regard the ending as an important part of the story and not just a quick sentence to 'wrap it up'.

A parable: the main points and **A parable: a modern version** (pages 34–35) consolidate the children's skills in recognising the key events in a story. They are based on a well-known biblical parable, for which the children plan a re-telling in a present-day context. The eight main points in the story are: i) the younger son asks for his inheritance; ii) his father agrees to give it to him; iii) the younger son spends all his money on clothes and having fun; iv) when he has no money left he has to work in very harsh conditions; v) he is sorry and decides to go home; vi) he goes home and his father celebrates; vii) his elder brother is jealous; viii) their father explains that he is rejoicing because he thought his son was dead, but he is not – he has come home and is sorry. The activity asks the children to re-tell the story in a different context; the headings will help them to separate the story into paragraphs.

Suspense... (page 36) develops the children's ability to recognise the ways in which writers create an effect or atmosphere. The activity sheet provides suggestions as to the ways in which they can create this atmosphere in their own writing.

A letter from a character (page 37) develops the children's ability to consider a situation in a story from different points of view and to present a point of view in the form of a 'first person' account. It also focuses their attention on the evidence in the story about a character.

Mystery story: cards (page 38) is a set of characters and settings to stimulate the children's ideas for a mystery story.

Mystery story: chapters (page 39) provides a framework for planning long stories split into chapters. Suggestions are made for the type of contents which might be included in each chapter.

Lively language (page 40) is about the ways in which well-chosen words can convey a great deal of meaning. It is linked with sentence-level work on adjectives, adverbs and interesting verbs. The children should also learn, from their reading, how a verb can create an effect without the use of adverbs (for example, 'trees frowned').

In **A strange sight!** (page 41) the children continue a poem with a repetitive pattern, the opening lines of which encourage them to be imaginative – to invent and describe strange sights. The complete poem can be found in several books, including *The Poetry Book* (Fiona Waters, Dolphin).

Write a rhythm (page 42) provides a starting point from which the children can write a performance poem. The starting point is the rhythm of a song from the traditional Inuit culture, in which hunting plays a prominent part in survival: to win a bride the Inuit boy in the song has to catch a seal to show that he can provide for her. The children will be able to read the words, albeit without understanding them, and to recognise the rhythm of the song – that of rowing a kayak.

Onomatopoeia (page 43) introduces the use of words which sound like their meanings. There are no 'right answers', but the following model answers might help: sizzling (sausages), swishing (broom), clinking (coins), rustling (leaves) and crunching (crisps).

Non-fiction: reading comprehension

Fiction or non-fiction? (page 44) focuses on the differences in style between fiction and non-fiction books: the children consider the type of language used, the tenses of verbs, the use of dialogue and the use of adjectives.

Finding information (page 45) develops the children's ability to use information sources efficiently. They begin by making explicit what they already know about specific aspects of a topic and then check this in books or other sources.

Key points (page 46) develops the children's ability to read and summarise a text. The six aspects of goalkeeping are: catching, cushioning, punching, deflecting, smothering and diving.

All about instructions (page 47) develops the children's awareness of the purposes of instructional texts. They could also classify a collection of instructional texts: recipes, maps and plans, washing instructions, rules and timetables. They should notice the features used to clarify the instructions: bullet points, numbered points, arrows, boxes, diagrams and keys.

Make a Chinese lantern (page 48) requires the children to read instructions for making a Chinese lantern, to make the lantern and to evaluate the way in which they followed the instructions.

Good or bad instructions (page 49) develops the children's ability to focus on specific aspects of the text.

All about letters (page 50) illustrates the six main purposes of letters: to complain, congratulate, recount, enquire, explain and comment. Before attempting this activity, the children should have had experience of reading different kinds of letters and recognising the clues which indicate their purposes.

How to use information books (page 51) helps the children to locate the information they want in reference books from a limited collection selected by the teacher (perhaps for the class library or topic loan). Having formulated a question, they think of key words connected with it. The teacher should model the way in which to use an index.

How to use a library (page 52) develops the children's skills in finding the appropriate section of the library and approaching their research in an organised way.

Non-fiction: writing composition

Making notes (page 53) develops the children's ability to scan reference books or CD-ROMs to locate information and to make notes. It provides a structure upon which they can organise their notes.

Writing a report (page 54) helps the children to structure a report in paragraphs. Making notes and then writing about the countries, rather than writing about them straight from the reference source, helps to avoid copying from the reference text.

Write your own instructions (page 55) develops the children's ability to write clear, easy-to-follow instructions. It also encourages them to organise instructions using lists, diagrams, bullet points and numbers.

Better notes (page 56) consolidates the children's skills in selecting the important words in a text and in making notes about the main aspects of the text for a given purpose (in this case to answer questions about it). Practice in note-making can be provided by having competitions to shorten a sentence to the fewest possible words which convey its meaning.

Organising notes: 1 and **2** (pages 57–58) provide structures to help the children to organise different kinds of notes. Notes in which chronological order is important can be organised on a time-line like the one provided in **Organising notes: 1** (the children will need help with the scale of a time-line), and notes which need to be classified can be organised using a two-column table, as in **Organising notes: 2**.

A formal letter (page 59) is a framework to help the children to structure a letter to someone they do not know.

A postcard (page 60) helps the children to reduce a text to the minimum which will convey the message of the full text.

A news report (page 61) provides an example of the different ways in which an event can be described. It is a recount (re-telling) of the rhyme *The Grand Old Duke of York* as a news report, using characters from other stories as well.

A glossary (page 62) contains words which the children will not understand: these are the ones which they should underline and look up in dictionaries, encyclopedias and other reference sources and include in the glossary.

A telephone directory (page 63) is another example of a familiar type of alphabetical text.

Sum it up! (page 64) challenges the children to write headlines which summarise each of the four texts. It develops their skills in reading a text and understanding its main point.

Glossary of terms used

alliteration The use of consecutive or nearly consecutive words which begin with the same phoneme, for example: *Two toads totally tired, four fat friars fishing for frogs.*

ambiguity More than one possible meaning.

calligram A poem in which the formation of the letters or shape of the words represents an aspect of the poem.

chronological writing Writing organised in terms of sequences of events or instructions.

couplet Two consecutive lines of poetry which are paired in length or rhyme.

genre A specific type of writing or other medium of communication, for example: legend, newspaper story or poem.

homograph A word with the same spelling as another, but a different meaning: for example, *hand* (of a human or a clock).

non-chronological writing Writing organised without reference to any time sequence.

onomatopoeia The use of words which echo sounds associated with their meaning: for example, *bang, boom, squeak.*

onset The initial consonant or consonant digraph sound of a word: for example, *big, chair.*

phoneme The smallest unit of sound in a word. A phoneme can be represented by one to four letters; for example, *bat, stay, stripe, eight.*

recount A text (or part of a text) written to describe an event or series of events for information or entertainment.

report A non-chronological text written to describe or classify.

rime The part of a syllable which contains the vowel and final consonant or consonant cluster, if there is one, for example: *cat, cow.*

Story settings

- **Underline the words which describe the smells of the potting sheds and outhouses.**

...she loved the potting sheds and outhouses, with their smells of lime and creosote and whitewash and oil and old grass shavings.

FROM *The Bongleweed* BY HELEN CRESSWELL

- **Complete these story settings.**

The dustbins were being emptied. He could smell

_____

_____

_____

She followed her mother past the market fruit stalls, breathing in the smells of _____

_____

_____

Now try this!

- **Write a story setting which describes a place you know.**

Think about what you would see, hear, smell and feel.

Teachers' note Read the passage with the children and invite them to describe the places where they have smelled creosote, whitewash, oil and grass shavings. The children could prepare for the activity by going into places at home and smelling them with their eyes closed.

Developing Literacy
Text Level Year 3
© A & C Black

Voices

The voices in a story can be the <u>narrator</u>, the <u>author</u> and the <u>characters</u>.

- **Read the passage.**
- **Underline each voice in a different colour.**
- **Complete the key.**

Key

1. Narrator

Mr Twit was furious. 'As there are no birds for my pie tonight,' he shouted, 'then it'll have to be boys instead!' He started to climb the ladder. 'Boy Pie might be better than Bird Pie,' he went on, grinning horribly. 'More meat and not so many tiny little bones!'

The boys were terrified. 'He's going to boil us!' cried one of them.

'He'll stew us alive!' wailed the second one.

'He'll cook us with carrots!' cried the third.

But the fourth little boy, who had more sense than the others, whispered, 'Listen, I've just had an idea...'

FROM *The Twits* BY ROALD DAHL

- **How many voices are there in the passage?** ☐

- **Work with a group.**
- **Read the passage aloud.**

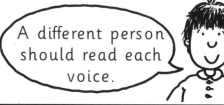

A different person should read each voice.

Teachers' note Ask the children how they can spot the words which are spoken. How do they know who says them? How can they spot the words of the narrator? Before reading the whole passage aloud each member of the group should be allocated a 'voice' and encouraged to read with expression. They should all be aware of when each voice begins and ends.

Developing Literacy
Text Level Year 3
© A & C Black

The Gingerbread Man: a play

- **Read this scene.**
- **Underline**
  - **the names of the characters in** red
  - **what the characters say in** blue
  - **the stage directions in** green .

A kitchen. An old woman rolls out dough and cuts out a gingerbread man. She places it on a baking tray and puts it in the oven and then washes up.

Old woman: (sniffing) Mmm! That smells good.

(Old woman takes the gingerbread man out of the oven.)

What a yummy-looking gingerbread man. The children can have him for tea.

Gingerbread man: (looking up) Oh, no they can't. No one will have me for tea!

(Gingerbread man jumps down and runs off.)

Old woman: Stop, stop!

Gingerbread man: (still running) No, I won't stop, and you can't catch me.

- **Write the next scene of the play. In this scene, an old man and the children come to help the old woman.**

Teachers' note Provide a copy of *The Gingerbread Man* to which the children can refer when writing the next scene. Different groups could write successive scenes so that the class has a complete playscript. If possible, find time for the groups to take turns to enact their scenes in the correct order, perhaps with younger children as an audience.

Developing Literacy
Text Level Year 3
© A & C Black

Story openings

What information can you find from the opening of a story?

- **Read these openings.**
- **Complete the chart.**

2 Football, football, football – Dave Brown was mad about football.

FROM *One Nil*
BY TONY BRADMAN

1 A man called Mr Jones and his wife lived near the sea.

FROM *A Necklace of Raindrops*
BY JOAN AIKEN

4 Meet Wizziwig, the greatest inventor the world has ever known. Well, actually, the world does not know about Wizziwig yet.

3 Streaker is a mixed-up kind of dog.

FROM *The Hundred-Mile-An-Hour Dog*
BY JEREMY STRONG

FROM *Wizziwig and the Weather Machine*
BY GERALDINE McCAUGHREAN

Story	Characters	Setting (if known)
1		
2		
3		
4		

- **Read the openings of two other stories.**
- **Make another chart to show the information you find.**

Teachers' note The children do not need to have read the stories featured before they tackle this activity. A display-sized version of the chart could be made on which the children record what they find out from the openings of other stories.

Developing Literacy
Text Level Year 3
© A & C Black

Story theme: good and evil

- Complete the chart.

Title	Good characters	Bad characters	Did good or evil win?	How did it win?
Snow White and the Seven Dwarfs	Snow White The Dwarfs The Woodcutter The Prince	The Wicked Queen		
Sleeping Beauty				
Cinderella				
Hansel and Gretel				

Include all kinds of stories, for example, myths and legends.

- Make another chart.
- Use it to record other stories about good and evil.

Now try this!

Teachers' note Provide copies of the stories to which the children can refer if necessary. Ask them how they know whether the characters are good or evil: they should use evidence from the text to justify their opinions (see also page 14).

Developing Literacy
Text Level Year 3
© A & C Black

Describing a character

- **Read the passage.**
- **Circle the words in the word-bank which you think describe Androcles. Use a different colour for each word.**
- **In the same colours, <u>underline</u> the words in the passage which made you think that.**

Word-bank

angry

brave

clever

foolish

funny

kind

lazy

strong

weak

Androcles hated being a slave. He never had enough to eat. He thought it wrong that his master could make him work and work without pay. He wanted to be free. One day he broke free from his chains. He ran and ran until he was exhausted. He fell asleep in a cave. A noise woke him. It was a lion. He was in its den! The lion roared at him. 'This is the end of me,' thought Androcles, 'but I would rather die than be a slave.' Then he saw that the lion's paw was bleeding. 'Keep still, and I shall help you,' he said to the lion.

FROM THE OLD LEGEND *Androcles and the Lion*

- **Describe another story character.**
- **Write six words or phrases from the story which tell you what the character is like.**

Teachers' note The text could be introduced as a guided reading activity during which any difficult words are discussed. The children might use the same evidence to support different views, for example: some might think Androcles was foolish for talking to a lion, while others might think he was brave. Encourage them to discuss their different views.

Developing Literacy
Text Level Year 3
© A & C Black

Penfriend characters

Imagine that a story character is looking for a penfriend.

- **Fill in the form for the character.**

Name_____

Human or animal_____

Male or female_____

 In this column, write how you know the answers.

Interests_____	_____
_____	_____
_____	_____
Personal qualities _____	_____
_____	_____
_____	_____
Special talents _____	_____
_____	_____

 **Now try this!**

- **Work in a group.**
- **Read one another's forms.**
- **Choose a penfriend for your character.**
- **Explain why you chose this character.**

Teachers' note The children could store their characters' profiles in a database which they could search for 'key words' (such as interests) to find a compatible penfriend for him or her. Some of them might be able to say why dissimilar characters could become penfriends (for example, the Wolf and a Little Pig could learn to understand one another).

Developing Literacy
Text Level Year 3
© A & C Black

Story review

- **Shade the balloons to show how good you thought a story was.**
- **Write the reasons why you thought this on the chart.**

Title _____

Author _____

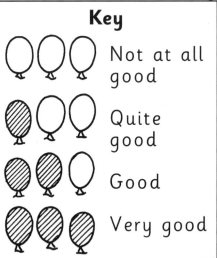

Key

Not at all good

Quite good

Good

Very good

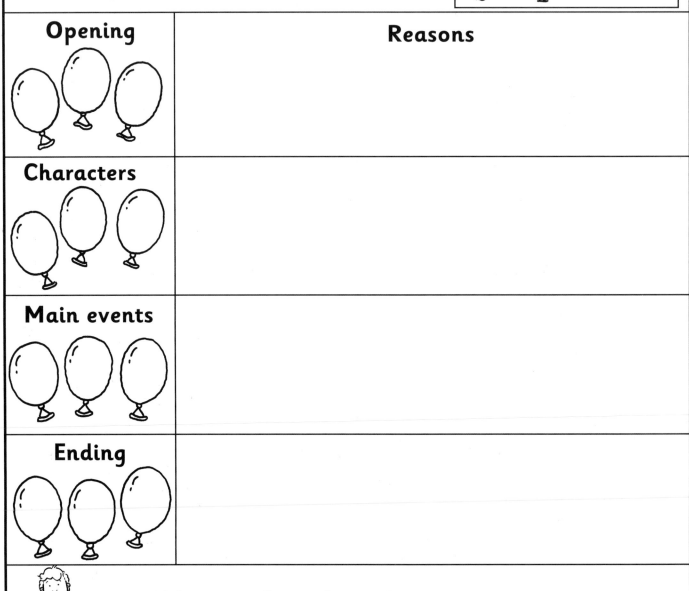

Opening	Reasons
Characters	
Main events	
Ending	

Now try this!

- **Write a review of another story you have read.**

Teachers' note Use this page with stories the children have read within the range suggested for Terms 2 and 3. They could compare their opinions about a story with those of others in the class, noting the reasons for their differing opinions.

Developing Literacy
Text Level Year 3
© A & C Black

Atmosphere

- **Read the passage.**
- **(Circle) the words in the word-bank which describe the atmosphere of the passage.**
- **Underline the words in the passage which create this atmosphere.**

Word-bank

boredom
dread
excitement
fear
fun
happiness
loneliness
mystery
sadness
sleepiness
waiting
wondering

As it began to grow dusk the huge black clouds rolled up in the distance, and the air grew very still and quiet. Now that all the work was done the fisher people gathered in groups on the shingle to wait. They talked in low excited whispers, rather frightened by the breathless silence.

FROM *The Little Sea Horse* BY HELEN CRESSWELL

Now try this!

- **Re-write the passage to give a joyful atmosphere.**
- **Change the words which you underlined.**

Use a thesaurus to add to the words in the word-bank.

Word-bank

bobbed	chatted	danced	fluffy	lively
carefree	cheerful	excited	happy	noisy

Teachers' note The passage could be read during a guided reading session, during which any difficult words are discussed. The children could compare their responses, noting the reasons for any differences.

**Developing Literacy
Text Level Year 3
© A & C Black**

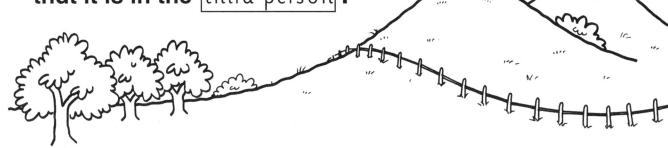

- **Read the passage.**
- **Underline the words which tell you that it is in the** third person **.**

When <u>Gulliver</u> awoke, <u>he</u> could not move. Dozens of cords fastened him to the ground. Even his hair was pegged to the ground so that he could not turn his head. After a while he felt something creeping along his leg and up his body. It stopped at his chin. To his astonishment, he saw a tiny human being.

FROM *Gulliver's Travels* BY JONATHAN SWIFT

- **Check your answers with a partner.**

Now try this!

- **Re-write the passage in the** first person **. Change the words which you underlined.**

Example: When I awoke, I could not move.

Teachers' note The children should first have had experience of comparing texts written in the first and third persons. Introduce the activity by reading short extracts from texts in each person and then ask the children to identify the person and to say how they knew.

Developing Literacy
Text Level Year 3
© A & C Black

Real life and fiction

- **Read the two passages.**

1.

Two horses escaped from the Priory stables today. They caused chaos among motorists and pedestrians in Top Street. One horse leapt over the barrier of the car park before being halted by a bystander. The other was on the run for an hour before the RSPCA managed to catch it outside the chip shop in Low Road.

2.

'Watch out! Horses!' yelled the man in the yellow raincoat as we trotted up Low Road. 'Nonsense,' laughed a small woman with grey hair. Then she heard the clip clop of our hooves. 'Aagh!' she screamed and dived into a doorway. The driver of a sports car shook his fist after Molly as she overtook him. I thought she would follow me. I could smell chips. Not many horses like chips, but I do. And that was what got me into trouble… an RSPCA officer was waiting for me in the doorway of the chip shop.

- **Which passage is fiction?** ☐
- **List the words which show this.**

_____

_____

Now try this!

- **Talk to a partner about the other differences between the passages.**
- **List these differences.**

Think about punctuation and dialogue.

Teachers' note The children should notice that the fiction text uses words which create an effect while the real-life account reports the facts. They should notice the use of dialogue in the fiction text and the differences in punctuation between the two texts (the fiction text uses exclamation marks, whereas the real-life text does not).

Developing Literacy
Text Level Year 3
© A & C Black

Use a dictionary.

• **Read these lines from poems about snails.**

1

With horns outstretched and pointed tail
Comes the grey and noiseless snail.
On ivy stems she clambers down,
Carrying her house of brown.
Safe in the dark, no greedy eye
Can her tender body spy,
While she herself, a hungry thief,
Searches out the freshest leaf.

FROM *The Snail* BY JAMES REEVES

2

Ye little snails
With slippery tails
Who noiselessly travel
Along this gravel,
By a silvery path of slime unsightly,
I learn that you visit my pea-rows nightly.

I give you this warning,
That, every morning,
I'll strictly examine the pods;
And if one I hit on,
With slaver or spit on,
Your next meal will be with the gods.

FROM *Remonstrance with the Snails* (ANONYMOUS)

Teachers' note Use these poems with the activity on page 21. Read each poem with the children and ask them what the poet thinks of snails: does he or she like them, find them interesting or think they are a nuisance? Ask them how they know. They should support their views by quoting words from the poems.

Developing Literacy
Text Level Year 3
© A & C Black

What do the two poems tell you?

- **Complete the chart.**

	✓ or ✗		Words or phrases which tell me this	
	Poem 1	Poem 2	Poem 1	Poem 2
The poet knows what snails eat.	✓	✓	leaf	pea-rows
The poet knows when snails feed.				
The poet knows how snails move.				
The poet has listened to snails.				
The poet wants to get rid of the snails.				
The poet enjoys gardening.				
The poet is talking to any reader.				
The poet is talking to the snails.				
The poem is a description.				
The poem is a warning.				

Now try this!

- **In which person is each poem written?**
- **How can you tell?**

Teachers' note Use this with page 20. It provides a framework on which the children can organise their views about the poems.

Developing Literacy
Text Level Year 3
© A & C Black

Bird words

- **Read the poem. Imagine the sounds and movements of the birds.**

The wild duck startles like a sudden thought,
And heron slow as if it might be caught;
The flopping crows on weary wings go by,
And greybeard jackdaws noising as they fly;
The crowds of starlings whizz and hurry by
And darken like a cloud the evening sky.

FROM *Autumn Birds* BY JOHN CLARE

- **Underline in red the words in the poem which tell you how each bird moves.**

- **Underline in blue the words which tell you the sound it makes.**

- **Complete the chart.**

Description	Bird	Key words from poem
Flaps its wings lazily	crow	flopping, weary wings
Buzzes about in huge flocks		
Takes off suddenly		
Makes a noise as it flies		
Takes off slowly		

- **Write a sentence that describes each of two of the birds in the poem.**
  Describe what you would see and hear.

Teachers' note To introduce the activity read the extract aloud with the children and ask them to describe the movement of the duck: which word in the poem tells them how it moves? At other times, they could observe birds and make notes about their sounds and movements: in class they could brainstorm words which describe the birds or suggest how they move.

Developing Literacy
Text Level Year 3
© A & C Black

Perform a poem

- **Read the first four verses of the poem aloud.**

- **Underline the words which you stressed.**

- **Read the last verse.**

- **Which word is stressed in the last line? Underline it.**

'Quack!' said the billy-goat.
  'Oink!' said the hen.
'Miaow!' said the little chick
  Running in the pen.

'Hobble-gobble!' said the dog.
  'Cluck!' said the sow.
'Tu-whit tu-whoo!' the donkey said.
  'Baa!' said the cow.

'Hee-haw!' the turkey cried.
  The duck began to moo.
All at once the sheep went,
  'Cock-a-doodle-doo!'

The owl coughed and cleared his
                              throat
  And he began to bleat.
'Bow-wow!' said the cock
  Swimming in the leat.

'Cheep-cheep!' said the cat
  As she began to fly.
'Farmer's been and laid an egg –
  That's the reason why.'

'Quack!' Said the Billy-goat BY CHARLES CAUSLEY

- **Work in a group.**
- **Plan a performance of the poem. Think about:**

Now try this!

actions

voices – who will read each voice

sound effects

how you will read the last line

Teachers' note Discuss the type of poem this is – a humorous poem. Can the children explain what makes it funny? How will this affect their performance of the poem? As well as underlining the stressed words, they could circle the rhyming words and notice that the stressed words do not rhyme. (See also page 24.)

**Developing Literacy
Text Level Year 3
© A & C Black**

Performance planner

Title of poem _____

Poet _____

Mood (for example, happy, funny, sad or thoughtful)	**Rhythm** (for example, walking, marching, rocking or skipping)	**Speed** (for example, slow, medium or fast)

Voices	Who will read it	Actions
		Sound effects

Teachers' note This sheet is designed for use with the poem on page 23, but it can also can be used to help the children to plan performances of other poems (although few others will have so many voices). The children could have a 'background' of muted animal noises, each one introduced as the animal appears in the poem, until all the animals are making their sounds.

Developing Literacy
Text Level Year 3
© A & C Black

Riddles

- **Match the riddles to the pictures.**

Riddle	1	2	3	4	5	6
Picture						

1

It goes through the mud
And along the path,
But leaves only one track.

2

Thirty white horses
On two red hulls.
Now they stamp,
Now they champ,
Now they stand still.

a   b   c   d   e   f

3

As round as an apple,
As deep as a pail;
It will only cry
If you pull its tail.

4

She has a white dress
and a red nose;
No feet nor hands.
The longer she stands
The shorter she grows.

5

I have the name of a man
But I'm as small as a mouse;
When winter comes I love to be
With my red front near the house.

6

Higher than a house,
Higher than a tree,
Whatever can it be?

Now try this!

- **Write a riddle for one of these.**

| a worm | a clock | a bubble |

Work with a partner.

Teachers' note Model an example with the children: for example, 'I have a tongue, but no mouth and I never eat' (show them a lace-up shoe and point out the tongue). For the extension activity they could brainstorm what they know about each thing in the list, for example: a worm has a mouth but no eyes; it breathes yet it has neither nose nor lungs.

Developing Literacy
Text Level Year 3
© A & C Black

Word-play

This poet had fun with words! • Read the poem.
- Underline five words with two meanings.
- Write the words and their meanings in the boxes.

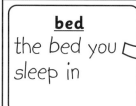

bed
the bed you sleep in

bed
the bottom of a river

Have you ever seen a sheet on a river <u>bed</u>?
Or a single hair on a hammer's head?
Has the foot of a mountain any toes?
And is there a pair of garden hose?

Does the needle ever wink its eye?
Why doesn't the wing of a building fly?
Can you tickle the ribs of a parasol?
Or open the trunk of a tree at all?

Are the teeth of a rake ever going to bite?
Have the hands of a clock any left or right?
Can the garden plot be deep and dark?
And what is the sound of a birch's bark?

Have you ever seen? (ANONYMOUS)

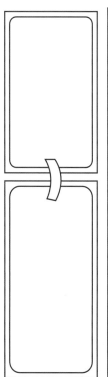
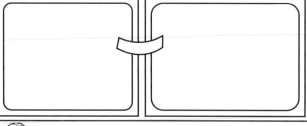
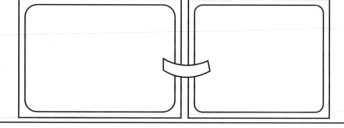

Now try this!

- Write four other words you know which have two or more meanings. Write the meanings.
- Write questions about the words to use in a poem.

Teachers' note Model the first example of word-play with the children: why does the poet ask about sheets on a river bed? (The children will know about sheets on a bed; but what is the bed of a river?) The extension activity provides an opportunity for them to think up word-plays of their own (it can be linked with work on homographs and homonyms).

Developing Literacy
Text Level Year 3
© A & C Black

- **Read the calligrams.**

- **Write calligrams in these shapes.**

- **Read this nursery rhyme calligram.**

- **Write your own calligram for a nursery rhyme.**

Teachers' note Collect and display other examples of calligrams and ask the children to prepare for this work by collecting examples of calligrams from poetry books and advertisements in magazines.

Developing Literacy
Text Level Year 3
© A & C Black

Alliteration

- **Read the poem aloud.
  Listen to the sounds of the words.**

- **Underline the phonemes
  with alliteration. Use a
  different colour for each
  different phoneme.**

Alliteration means having the same sound.

Rumbling in the chimneys,
   Rattling at the doors,
Round the roofs and round the roads
   The rude wind roars;
Raging through the darkness,
   Raving through the trees,
Racing off again across
   The great grey seas.

Windy Nights BY RODNEY BENNET

Now try this!

- **Write in the gaps
  words with alliteration.**

Think of words which make sense together.

Example: <u>sl</u>imy <u>sl</u>ugs

seven _____   _____ daisies

_____ towers   lovely _____

bubbling _____   _____ neighbours

_____ children   playful _____

Teachers' note Read the poem with the children. They could look for examples in other poems of 'almost alliteration' which have a similar effect, when read aloud, as true alliteration.

**Developing Literacy
Text Level Year 3
© A & C Black**

What did they say?

- **Follow the picture story.**
- **Think about what is happening.**
- **In the speech bubbles, write the dialogue.**

- **Write the story without the pictures.**

  Use quotation marks.   " "

Teachers' note Model the writing of the first speech bubble with the children. Ask them to work out from the picture how the boy feels and what he might say (the next picture gives a clue – something makes his mother come into the room). For the extension activity, they can make notes about the setting of the story and some of the words they might use to create its atmosphere.

Developing Literacy
Text Level Year 3
© A & C Black

Script planner

- **Plan a scene for a play.**

Who are the characters?	Setting (include what you see and hear)	

Character's name	What he or she does	What he or she says

- **Use your notes to help you to write the script for the play.**

Teachers' note The children should first complete page 29 in which they write a dialogue in speech bubbles for a picture story and, if they complete the extension activity, as text with dialogue in speech marks. All the information they need is in the picture, but the children might like to continue the story.

Developing Literacy
Text Level Year 3
© A & C Black

Collecting ideas for a story

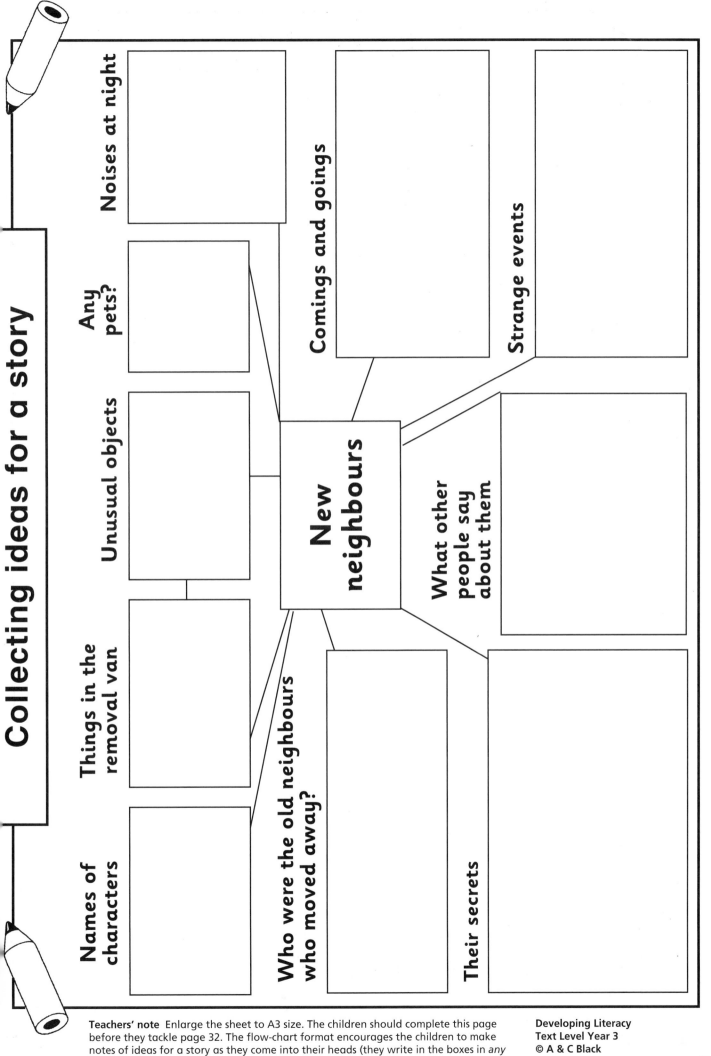

Noises at night

Any pets?

Unusual objects

Things in the removal van

Names of characters

Comings and goings

Strange events

New neighbours

What other people say about them

Who were the old neighbours who moved away?

Their secrets

Teachers' note Enlarge the sheet to A3 size. The children should complete this page before they tackle page 32. The flow-chart format encourages the children to make notes of ideas for a story as they come into their heads (they write in the boxes in *any* order) before the more formal structuring of the story.

Developing Literacy
Text Level Year 3
© A & C Black

31

Writing a story opening

How can you improve this story opening?

- **Re-write the sentences.**

Add more sentences if you need to.

---

1. Chloe saw a van next door.
2. People were carrying furniture and other things into the house.
3. The new neighbours drove on to the driveway and got out of the car.

---

1. _____

_____

_____

_____

_____

Where was Chloe? What was she doing when she saw the van? Describe the road and houses.

2. _____

_____

_____

_____

_____

What furniture and what other things did the people carry into the house? How did they carry them?

3. _____

_____

_____

_____

What did the new neighbours look like? How many of them were there? How old were they?

Now try this!

- **Re-draft the story opening. Make it show what Chloe was thinking and feeling.**

Teachers' note Use this activity sheet with the completed page 31. The children should first complete page 12 which provides examples of story openings and draws attention to the ways in which they introduce characters and set the scene for a story.

Developing Literacy
Text Level Year 3
© A & C Black

Writing a story ending

- **Use the chart to plan the ending of a story.**

Problems to resolve	The resolution

Events to explain	The explanation

The future of the main character

Something for the reader to think about

Teachers' note Read the ending of a story as a shared text. Is it a satisfying ending? In what way? Does it: resolve problems? explain mysteries? give an idea of what might happen next? leave the reader with something to think about? The children should take these considerations into account when planning their own story endings.

Developing Literacy
Text Level Year 3
© A & C Black

A parable: the main points

- **Read the parable** *The Lost Son*.

- **Write the main points of the story in the table.**
  Write in note form.

This parable is in the Bible, in Luke, chapter 15, verses 11–32.

1. Man has two sons who will inherit his property. Younger son wants his share now.	**5.**
2. Father gives younger son his share.	**6.**
3.	**7.**
4.	**8.**

Now try this!

- **Use your notes to plan a modern version of the parable.**

You can change the setting and other details.

Teachers' note Provide copies of the Bible in which the children can read the *Parable of the Lost Son*. Discuss the message of the parable, which Jesus used to teach people that God rejoices when someone who has done wrong is sorry. The children should be able to identify eight main points in the story (see Introduction, page 7). See also page 35.

Developing Literacy
Text Level Year 3
© A & C Black

A parable: a modern version

- **Write a modern version of** *The Lost Son* **as a newspaper report.**

The Holy Bible
Luke, chapter 15
verses 11–32

Galilee Times

Only
6 shekels

LOST SON RETURNS

INHERITANCE DEMANDED	THOUGHTS OF HOME
FATHER GIVES IN	A GREAT PARTY
A LIFE OF LUXURY	JEALOUS BROTHER COMPLAINS
POVERTY AND SORROW	A FATHER'S WISE WORDS

Teachers' note See also page 34, in which the children will have identified the main points of the story. The emphasis here is on the re-telling of the parable in a different context. The children could use computer software which provides a newspaper format. They could also use a computer to design and print their reports.

Developing Literacy
Text Level Year 3
© A & C Black

Suspense...

- ## Read the passage.

The library was pitch black and very eerie. Harry lit a lamp to see his way along the rows of books. The lamp looked as if it was floating along in mid-air, and even though Harry could feel his arm supporting it, the sight gave him the creeps.

The Restricted Section was right at the back of the library. Stepping carefully over the rope which separated these books from the rest of the library, he held up his lamp to read the titles.

They didn't tell him much. Their peeling, faded gold letters spelled words in languages Harry couldn't understand. Some had no title at all. One book had a dark stain on it that looked horribly like blood. The hairs on the back of Harry's neck prickled. Maybe he was imagining it, maybe not, but he thought a faint whispering was coming from the books, as though they knew someone was there who shouldn't be.

FROM *Harry Potter and the Philosopher's Stone* BY J K ROWLING

- ## Complete the chart to show how the author builds up suspense.

1. What the place is like	2. What Harry does
3. What Harry sees and feels	4. What Harry does next
5. What Harry sees (or feels, hears or smells) next	6. The strange things Harry imagines

- ## Plan a passage for your own story.

Think about how you will create suspense.

Teachers' note Read the passage with the children and ask them to identify the words which create suspense. In the extension activity they should plan, in note form, a passage of their own which builds up suspense. (See also page 17, which concentrates on the language used to create an atmosphere.)

Developing Literacy
Text Level Year 3
© A & C Black

A letter from a character

Choose an event from a story.
- Write a letter about the event. Write as if you are a character who was there.
- You could write it to another story character.

Don't choose the main character.

Character's address

_____

_____

_____

Date

_____

Dear

_____

_____

_____

_____

_____

_____

_____

_____

_____

Yours sincerely

_____

Teachers' note It is important to consider characters other than the main one in a story. You could read a shared text and ask the children from which character's point of view the story is written. Ask them to think of the feelings and opinions of any character and what might be important to them. They should justify what they say with evidence from the text.

Developing Literacy
Text Level Year 3
© A & C Black

Mystery story: cards

A ruined castle

Only the dried-up moat and the crumbling walls of the castle can still be seen. But there are dungeons buried under the ground.

A deserted railway station

The broken paving stones on the platform are overgrown with moss and the roof has gone from the old waiting-room. The tracks are rusted.

An empty shop

All the shops in the main shopping street are packed with people – except one. Many years ago large boards were nailed across its door and windows, and have never been removed.

A tower

In a field stands a round brick tower with tiny high-up slit windows with glass in them. There is also a padlocked door. The door is painted, the windows are clean and the lock is oiled, but no one is ever seen to go inside.

A patch of grass

The bright green lawn in the park is the pride of the town, but in the middle, there is an unusual square patch. It is about a metre along each side and deep emerald green. This is always a little longer than the other grass and has a silky soft feel.

A red glow

Under the street lights the road signs shine greeny-yellow at night – except one. It glows bright red, as if illuminated from inside.

A man with a long coat

His coat covers his shoes and brushes along the ground behind him. It fits him perfectly in every other way, from its crisply folded collar to its neatly stitched hem. And he wears it whatever the weather.

A noise at sunset

It begins every evening just as the sun is setting, a gentle, low moaning sound which becomes higher and higher until it is almost a soft scream. And then, when the sun goes down, it stops, suddenly.

An old clock

The clock has hung on the wall in the hall for as long as anyone can remember. It never stops, but no one winds it. It is silent all year, except for 31st October – when it strikes the hours.

The pocket

The old raincoat hangs from a peg behind the door. No one owns it, but people put it on to put the rubbish out or walk the dog. It has a very deep pocket. Its many wearers have never reached right down to the bottom of the pocket – until today.

The bridge

People walk under the plain brick bridge, they drive under it and shelter under it in the rain, but they hardly ever look at its arched walls. About two metres up is a hole which burrows into the railway embankment.

The bottle from the sea

A dark green bottle, the colour of seaweed, was wedged between the rocks. It had a cork pushed into the top and inside it was a piece of paper.

Teachers' note Laminate a copy of the page for re-use and cut out the cards. The children choose one card as the starting point for a mystery story. They could brainstorm ideas suggested by the card, using a flow chart like the one on page 31, before planning a long story which is split into chapters (see page 39).

Developing Literacy
Text Level Year 3
© A & C Black

Mystery story: chapters

- **Choose a mystery card from page 38.**
- **Plan a mystery story in five chapters.**

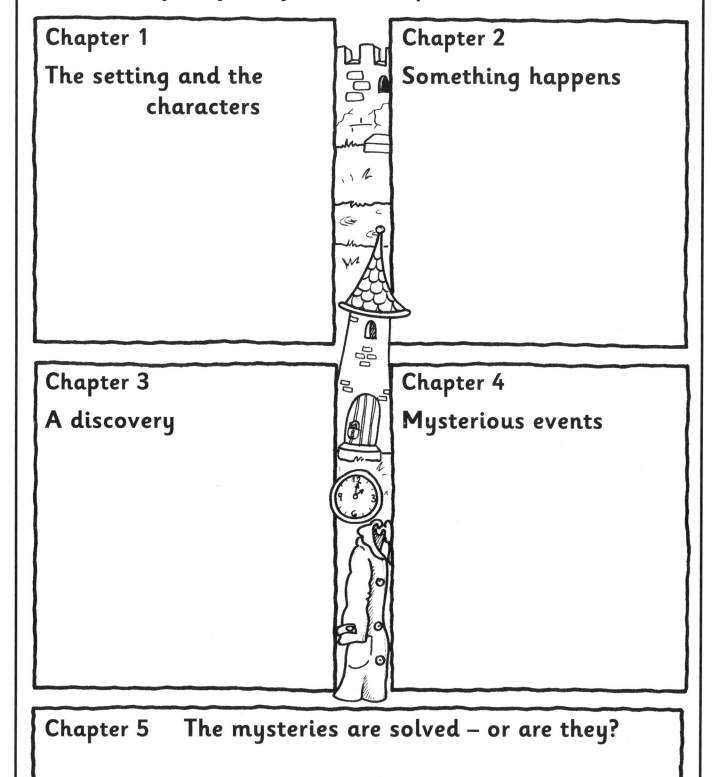

Chapter 1

The setting and the characters

Chapter 2

Something happens

Chapter 3

A discovery

Chapter 4

Mysterious events

Chapter 5   The mysteries are solved – or are they?

Teachers' note Use this activity with page 38. Having generated ideas for a mystery story (see also page 31), the children can use this framework to help them to plan the main events of the story.

Developing Literacy
Text Level Year 3
© A & C Black

Lively language

- **Use this page to record interesting words and phrases you have read.**

> Here are some examples to start you off.

Words and phrases	Image
the <u>mighty</u> cliffs	enormous cliffs
trees <u>frowned</u> on each side	dark, gloomy trees

- **Copy three sentences from books which contain** interesting verbs **and** interesting adjectives.

> Underline the verbs and adjectives.

Teachers' note Encourage the children to notice any interesting words and phrases which they come across in their reading. This page provides a chart on which to record them and to describe the effects which they create.

Developing Literacy Text Level Year 3 © A & C Black

A strange sight!

- **Read the lines from the poem.**
- **Underline the rhyming words.**
- **Continue the poem in your own words.**

Use a different colour for each pair of rhyming words.

I saw a peacock with a fiery tail
I saw a blazing comet drop down hail
I saw a cloud with ivy circled round
I saw a sturdy oak creep on the ground
I saw an ant swallow a whale
I saw _____ ← This line should rhyme with 'whale'.

_____ ←
_____ ← These two lines should rhyme.

_____

_____

_____

_____

_____

FROM *I saw* (ANONYMOUS)

Now try this!

- **Write an ending for the poem.**

The original poem ends:
I saw a man who saw these too
And says though strange they are all true.

Teachers' note Read the lines aloud with the children and ask them to identify the rhyming words. Model the first example with them and ask them to think up the most unlikely sights to describe. The extension activity encourages them to write an unexpected ending.

Developing Literacy Text Level Year 3 © A & C Black

Write a rhythm

- **Read this traditional Inuit song and its story.**

 **The song**

 **The story**

Chorus:
Okki-tokki-unga, okki-tokki-unga,
Hey, Missa Day, Missa Doh, Missa Day,
Okki-tokki-unga, okki-tokki-unga,
Hey, Missa Day, Missa Doh, Missa Day.

Verse:
Hexa cola misha woni,
Hexa cola misha woni,
Hexa cola misha woni.

1	2
The boy looks for a seal.	 He harpoons a seal and hauls it into his kayak.

3	4
 He waves to his girlfriend.	 The kayak overturns. The boy swims ashore.

- **Write your own words to the rhythm of the verse. They should make sense.**

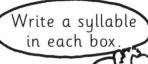 Write a syllable in each box.

Verse 1

Hex	a	co	la	mi	sha	wo	ni

Verse 2

Verse 3

Verse 4

 Now try this!

- **Read your verses aloud. Repeat each line three times.**

 Don't forget the chorus.

Teachers' note Read the chorus and the verse (while the children clap the rhythm). Explain that the same verse is repeated four times while part of the story is mimed. (During the chorus, the rowing of the kayak is mimed.) Groups of children could perform their verses while others mime the story.

**Developing Literacy
Text Level Year 3
© A & C Black**

Onomatopoeia

- **Complete this poem using words which have onomatopoeia.**

If words have onomatopoeia, they sound like their meanings.

Who's that tapping? Tap-tap.

The joiner's tapping a hammer. Tap-tap.

Who's that clinking? Clink-clink.

The banker's clinking coins. Clink-clink.

Who's that squeaking? _____

The children are _____ the door._____

Who's that _____? _____

The cook's _____ sausages. _____

Who's that _____? _____

The cleaner's _____ a broom _____

Who's that _____? _____

The wind's _____ leaves. _____

Who's that _____? _____

It's me _____ crisps! _____

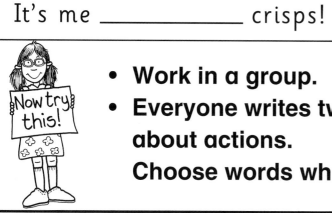

Now try this!

- **Work in a group.**
- **Everyone writes two lines of a poem about actions.**
Choose words which sound like the actions.

Teachers' note You could introduce the activity using a shared text which features onomatopoeia. Ask the children to collect examples of onomatopoeia which could be recorded on a wall-chart or database.

Developing Literacy
Text Level Year 3
© A & C Black

Fiction or non-fiction?

**Are these sentences from fiction
or non-fiction books?**

• **Write 'F' (fiction) or 'N' (non-fiction).**

Sentence	F or N	How I can tell
The cod is a sea fish.	N	This is a fact. It gives information about a real thing.
In AD 122 the Roman emperor, Hadrian, had a wall built across northern England.		
Clare pressed her eye to the keyhole and waited.		
"What's that?" gasped Mark.		
Mix together the flour, salt and butter.		
Hasanna loved the smell of the old, leather-bound books.		

Work with a partner.

• **Write definitions of a** `fiction book`
and `a non-fiction book` .

Teachers' note The children should first have had the opportunity to compare a range of fiction and non-fiction books and to discuss the layout features of each and the different types of language they use.

Developing Literacy
Text Level Year 3
© A & C Black

Finding information

- **Write what you know about snakes.**
- **Check your answers using information books or CD-ROMs.**

Use the contents, index, headings and sub-headings.

What I know...	What I found out
...about how snakes feed	
...about how snakes protect themselves	
...about snakes' skin	
...about baby snakes	

- **Write something else you know about snakes. Check it using an information book or CD-ROM.**

Now try this!

Teachers' note This activity can be used to extend work on a particular topic in another subject, where the teacher has specified the kind of information which the children are to find and has provided a collection of suitable reference books.

Developing Literacy
Text Level Year 3
© A & C Black

Key points

- **Read the passage.**

A goalkeeper can keep the ball out of the net in six different ways. To catch the ball above chest height, the goalkeeper's fingers are spread out with the thumbs behind the ball. To cushion a ball at chest height or below, the goalkeeper catches it and pulls it into the body. If the ball is too high to catch, the goalkeeper can punch it; to do this both fists are clenched tightly and held together and the wrists are kept firm. If the ball is too high to catch or punch, the goalkeeper can deflect it: he or she tips it over the bar with the palm of the hand. A very low ball can be smothered – covered with the body. The goalkeeper can dive to deflect, catch or smother a ball which is difficult to reach.

- **List the key points to show the ways a goalkeeper can save a ball.**

1. Above chest height, catch it.

2. _____

3. _____

4. _____

5. _____

6. _____

- **Re-write the text with a heading. Use a sub-heading for each key point.**

Draw a picture for each key point.

Teachers' note The children should decide what are the key points of the text: the six important pieces of information. In the extension activity their heading should summarise what the whole text is about.

Developing Literacy
Text Level Year 3
© A & C Black

All about instructions

Instructions tell you how, where or when to do something.

- ## What do these instructions tell people?

1 100% cotton wash separately

2 **Leek and potato soup**

Ingredients
2 large leeks
1 medium potato
25g butter
750 ml stock

Method
Slice the leeks into small rings. Cut the peeled potatoes into small cubes. Melt the butter in a large

3 Vitamin Tonic

Dose
Adults 10ml
three times a day

4 CARDIFF STREET PLAN

5 Mobile phone USERS' MANUAL

6 SCHOOL RULES
1. Be kind
2. Be polite
3. Walk, don't run in the

7 Safe places to cross roads
1. Crossing patrol
2. Zebra crossing

	What the instructions tell people
1	how to
2	
3	
4	
5	
6	
7	

Now try this!

- ## Look at other instructions. What do they tell you?

Title	What the text tells me

Record your findings on a chart.

Teachers' note The children should begin each answer with 'how to', having decided (perhaps with a partner) what is the purpose of the instructional text. They could collect, classify (according to purpose) and display everyday instructional texts such as labels indicating washing instructions, plans, tourist maps and rules.

Developing Literacy
Text Level Year 3
© A & C Black

Make a Chinese lantern

- **Read the instructions.**
- **Make a Chinese lantern.**

You need:
patterned paper
scissors
glue

1. Cut the paper into a rectangle and a strip.

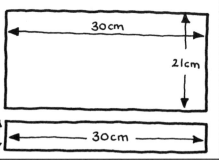

30cm
21cm
3cm
30cm

2.

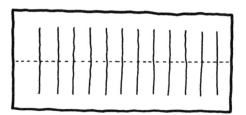
fold

Fold the rectangle in half lengthwise.

3.

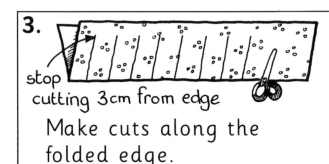
stop cutting 3cm from edge
Make cuts along the folded edge.

4.

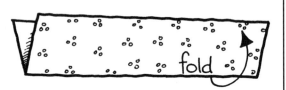

Open out the paper.

5. Bend the paper to make a cylinder. Glue the edges.

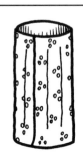

6. Glue on the strip of paper to make a handle.

- **How well did you follow the instructions? Colour a face.**

Very well

Quite well

Not very well

Now try this!

- **Underline any part of the instructions which**
  - **you missed out in** red
  - **you did not understand in** blue

Teachers' note Provide patterned paper (such as gift wrapping paper) so that the children can follow the numbered instructions to make the Chinese lantern. Encourage them to evaluate the way in which they followed the instructions.

Developing Literacy
Text Level Year 3
© A & C Black

Good or bad instructions

- **Read some instructions.**
- **Try following the instructions.**
- **Do the rocket test! Give the instructions a score for each question.**
- **Give reasons for your answers.**

 Colour the rockets.

1= lowest score
5= highest score

Title _____

Subject _____

Purpose _____

Reasons

How easy is it to read the instructions?

_____
_____
_____

How easy are they to understand?

_____
_____
_____

How attractive are they?

_____
_____
_____

How well ordered are they?

_____
_____
_____

- **How accurate is the text?**
Check it using other books or CD-ROMs.

Teachers' note The children could work in pairs on this activity. You could model the reading of an instructional text (perhaps for making something like a paper plane or a kite), by 'thinking aloud', for example: 'Now, what do I need?', 'Yes, here it says...', 'What do I do first?', 'No, it doesn't mean that...' Evaluate the instructions with the children.

Developing Literacy
Text Level Year 3
© A & C Black

All about letters

- **Match the letters to their purposes.**
  Complete the chart.

1

Dear Ian,

We were very pleased to hear about your exam results. You must have worked very hard.

2

Dear Sir or Madam,

I enclose the wrapper from a 'Softy' toffee bar. It was not at all soft as advertised, but as hard as nails.

3

Dear Editor,

I do like the new format of the *Daily Shout* – it is much easier to find the television guide now that it is on the back page.

Letter	Purpose	About what?
2	**to complain**	a hard toffee bar
	to congratulate	
	to recount	
	to enquire	
	to explain	
	to comment	

4

Dear Mrs Aske,

In answer to your questions about the new layout of the store:

· we installed frozen food units with doors because these help to keep the food at the right temperature.

5

Dear Megan,

We had a lovely time in Paris. We went to the top of the Eiffel Tower – we could see the whole city. After that we cruised along the River Seine.

6

Dear Sir or Madam,

I would be very grateful if you would send me details of hotels and tourist attractions in North Wales.

- **Read six other letters.**
- **Explain why they were written and what kind of reply the writer hoped to receive.**

Teachers' note Ask the children to think of letters they have written; to whom did they write and what were the purposes of the letters? During guided reading activities, they could read letters they have brought from home or which the teacher has supplied, and notice the type of language used in different kinds of letters.

Developing Literacy
Text Level Year 3
© A & C Black

How to use information books

My question _____

Key words to look for

Underline the first letter.

Title of book _____

Key words in alphabetical order	Pages to look at

Now try this!

- **Make notes which will help to answer your question.**

Teachers' note Provide a limited selection of information books in which the children can find the answer to a question. Model an example, explaining how you choose the key words and how you use an index, contents page and chapter headings to locate the pages which might help to answer the question. (Revise alphabetical order if necessary.)

Developing Literacy
Text Level Year 3
© A & C Black

How to use a library

My question

_____

The section of this library which will help me:

Red	**Fiction**		
Yellow	**Poetry**		
Dark blue	**Mathematics**	Purple	**History**
Orange	**Science and natural history**	Brown	**Geography**
		White	**Art**
Green	**Technology and inventions**	Magenta	**Music**
		Pale blue	**Sport**

Underline the library section.

The books which will help me:

Section name and colour code	Title	Author	Publisher

Teachers' note You could adapt the sheet to follow the classification system used in your school library. If possible, you could also take the children to a public library. Show them how to find the books in the library. They could learn about the Dewey Decimal System.

Developing Literacy
Text Level Year 3
© A & C Black

Making notes

- **Read the chart.**
- **Find the information about each country.**
- **Complete the chart with key words.**

Use information books or CD-ROMs.

	Ghana	Iceland
Location • Which continent is it in? • Is it near the Equator, Tropics or Pole? • Nearest seas or oceans		
Size and shape • Large or small compared with UK? • Long, thin or square? • Is it an island? • Nearest countries		
Main physical features • Mountains, deserts, glaciers, plains or forests?		

- **Choose one country and find out more about it.**
  Make notes about its climate, main industries and religions.

Now try this!

Teachers' note Provide reference sources from which the children can find the information. The process of note-making could first be modelled using a video about a country: the teacher makes notes on a flip-chart as the children watch the video. Then they could suggest improvements to the notes. Continued on page 54.

Developing Literacy
Text Level Year 3
© A & C Black

53

Writing a report

- **Draft a report about a country.
  Use your notes from page 53.**

Heading _____

	Paragraph 1 **Sub-heading: Location**
Write sentences about the continent and the part of the world the country is in. Write about the surrounding seas and oceans.	
	Paragraph 2 **Sub-heading: Size and shape**
Write sentences about the size and shape of the country, the countries it is near and if it is an island.	
	Paragraph 3 **Sub-heading: Main physical features**
Write sentences about any mountains, deserts, glaciers, plains and forests in the country.	
	Paragraph 4 **Sub-heading: Climate**
Write sentences about the seasons there: weather and hours of light and dark.	

Continue on a separate sheet if you need to.

Now try this!

- **Re-draft your report as a booklet
  with maps and pictures.**

Teachers' note The children should first complete page 53. The purpose of the report could be to present information about the chosen country to the rest of the class or to plan an audio-recording about the country.

**Developing Literacy
Text Level Year 3
© A & C Black**

Write your own instructions

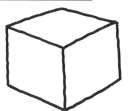

- **Write instructions for making a cube out of paper.**

How to make _____

You need:

- _____
- _____
- _____

- _____
- _____
- _____

1.

2.

3.

4.

- **Ask a friend to follow your instructions and evaluate them.**

Teachers' note Show the children how to make a paper cube. This could be linked with work in mathematics. Encourage them to use diagrams in their instructions. After the extension activity they could re-draft their instructions, improving any parts their partner could not follow.

Developing Literacy
Text Level Year 3
© A & C Black

Better notes

- **Read the passage and underline the important words about Viking crafts.**

Your notes can help you to answer questions about Viking crafts.

The Viking settlement of Jorvik (York)

There has been a settlement at York since the Romans built a fort there in the first century. Many of the buildings, walls and roads had been left to fall into ruins. In 866 the Vikings captured the city and repaired the Roman walls. They set out new streets there and built houses of wattle (woven sticks) with thatched roofs.

10,000 people were living in Jorvik by the year 1000. There were many craftspeople: jewellers who made silver and gold bracelets and rings, and amber, jet and glass beads; weavers and dyers who worked with woollen cloth; and leather-workers who made shoes, belts and even cups. Coins were stamped from gold, silver and copper; wooden bowls and cups were made; and combs, needles and other utensils were made from bone. Potters made clay pots for cooking.

The Vikings traded with European and Asian countries. Archaeologists have found coins and pieces of silk from Asia in the Jorvik settlement.

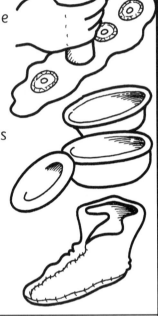

- **Write notes to help you remember the information.**

_____

_____

_____

_____

_____

- **Read your notes. Cross out any words you do not need.**

Now try this!

- **Ask a partner to write three questions about Viking crafts for you to answer.**
- **Answer them using only your notes.**

Teachers' note Read the first sentence with the children and ask them if it tells them about Viking crafts; do the same with each sentence until you reach one which provides this information. They should underline the words for the people, the things they made and the materials they used.

Developing Literacy
Text Level Year 3
© A & C Black

Organising notes: 1

- **Read the notes about the Romans in Britain.**
- **Write them in the correct order on the time-line.**

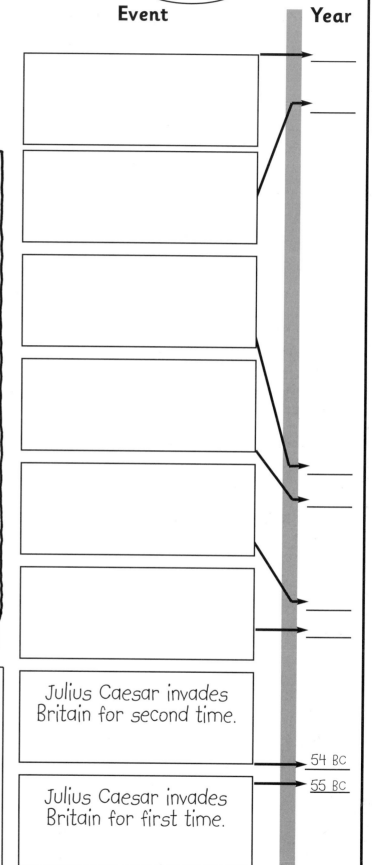

Time-line

Event   Year

54 BC	Julius Caesar invades Britain for second time
AD 143	Romans build Antonine Wall to defend Northumberland from Picts in Scotland
AD 410	Romans leave Britain
AD 382	Romans abandon Hadrian's Wall
AD 120 –126	Romans build Hadrian's Wall to keep out Picts from Scotland
AD 43	Claudius invades Britain
AD 60	Boudica leads rebellion against Romans in South of England
55 BC	Julius Caesar invades Britain for first time

Julius Caesar invades Britain for second time.

54 BC

Julius Caesar invades Britain for first time.

55 BC

Now try this!

- **Plan a book about the Romans in Britain. What other information do you need?**

Teachers' note Encourage the children to look for parts of the text which belong together (the first example is provided on the time-line). They could underline them in the same colour and then number them in the order in which they are to be written on the time-line. They could cross out each note once it is in the time-line.

Developing Literacy
Text Level Year 3
© A & C Black

Organising notes: 2

- **Read these replies from questionnaires about changing a school's holidays so that there would be four terms instead of three.**

It would make family holidays difficult where the children go to different schools.

Difficult for parents who are teachers at other schools.

It would be good – it would stop children getting bored in the long summer holiday.

It would be difficult for parents who have children at the nursery. Their holidays would be different and it would mean extra days of taking children to school.

Six-week holidays are too long. Children forget what they have learned. Shorter holidays would be better.

No good! We wouldn't be able to have our long annual holiday of five weeks in Scotland.

It would be better because teachers and children get tired at the end of a long term.

It would be difficult for teachers whose children go to other schools.

- **Write notes about the replies.**

Arguments for the change	Arguments against the change

- **Write a summary of the notes.**
  Say whether most people are for or against the change.

Teachers' note The children could work in pairs, deciding whether each 'reply' is for or against the change of the school's holidays. They could cross out each one as they write a summary of it on the table. This links with earlier work on note-making (see pages 53 and 56).

Developing Literacy
Text Level Year 3
© A & C Black

A formal letter

- **Draft a letter to an organisation which could help you with a school project.**

_____ → School address

_____

_____

_____ → Date

→ Name of person to whom you are writing

Dear _____

_____

_____

_____ → **Paragraph 1** Explain why you are writing.

_____

_____

_____

_____ → **Paragraph 2** List the kind of information which would be useful.

_____

_____

_____

_____ → **Paragraph 3** Thank the person for reading the letter and say that you look forward to hearing from him or her.

_____

_____

_____

_____

Yours sincerely

_____ → Your personal name and family name

Teachers' note To make it meaningful for the children, this activity could be linked with work in another subject. Provide an example of a letter (perhaps written by yourself) requesting information from someone. Point out to the children the paragraphs which explain why you are writing, which list the information required and which give a polite ending.

Developing Literacy
Text Level Year 3
© A & C Black

59

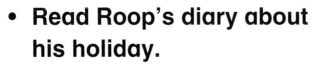

- **Read Roop's diary about his holiday.**
- **Help him decide what to write on a postcard to his friend May.**

May Brown lives in Luton. Her postcode is LU1 3EP. Her house is number 64 South Road.

Monday

Rain all day. Thunderstorm at night. Boring shopping with Mum + Dad. Pizza and greasy chips.

Tuesday

Rain again. Wish I could go to the beach. Bread at breakfast stale. Greasy chips.

Wednesday

Rain. Went on coach trip to Barcelona. Saw beautiful buildings: churches, art gallery. Bread stale again. More chips (greasy).

Thursday

Stale bread again – sunshine. Beach great. Played in sea with new friend, Sam. Greasy chips.

POSTCARD

Dear May

Roop's message →

May's name and address

Love from Roop

Teachers' note The children should first complete pages 53 and 56–58. The small size of the postcard challenges them to write as briefly as possible. Provide examples of postcards for them to read, pointing out the differences between them and formal letters (page 59), in particular that complete sentences need not be written.

Developing Literacy
Text Level Year 3
© A & C Black

A news report

- **Complete this newspaper report about The Grand Old Duke of York.**

INVASION SCARE

Military action on hill near York

by _____

Huge army on the move

About ten thousand soldiers were seen marching up and down the hills on Marston Moor, near York, yesterday.

Little Bo Peep, 8, said, 'My sheep were so scared, they ran away. I still haven't found them.'

Other local people described the movements of the army: 'There was a chap barking orders – really bossy, he was,' said Old Mother Hubbard, 103.

'_____
_____
_____
_____ ,
_____
said Tom the Piper's son, 10. Bobby Shaftoe, 87, a retired naval officer added _____
_____
_____
_____
_____

- **Re-write another nursery rhyme in the style of a newspaper report.**

Teachers' note This activity is intended to be fun. Read the text with the children, pointing out features such as the inclusion of people's ages (show them newspaper reports, which generally do this) and quotes from witnesses or interested parties.

Developing Literacy
Text Level Year 3
© A & C Black

A glossary

- **Read the passage.**
- **Underline the words which need to be in a glossary.**
- **Write the glossary.**

 Use a dictionary.

A glossary should be in alphabetical order.

Parts of the ancient skeleton were intact, including the skull, lower jaw and most of the vertebrae. The bones of one leg were missing and all those of the other leg were damaged: the tibia, fibula and patella. Most of the ribs were in fragments, as was the sternum. But the bones of the arms were in good condition. A pile of small bones was collected: probably the carpals and tarsals.

Glossary

carpal One of many small bones in the wrist.

_____
_____
_____
_____
_____
_____
_____
_____

_____
_____
_____
_____
_____
_____
_____
_____

Teachers' note Provide dictionaries and reference sources in which the children can look up the 'technical' words for the glossary. If necessary, revise alphabetical order, including the second letter.

Developing Literacy
Text Level Year 3
© A & C Black

A telephone directory

- **Write the Toytown telephone directory.**

Write the family name, then the personal name, then the address.

Telephone directories are in alphabetical order.

Bo Peep
2 Field Lane
Toytown
TO1 3BL

Mother Goose
3 Egg Street
Toytown
TO3 2BR

Jack Sprat
1 Meat Lane
Toytown
TO2 3AX

Jack Horner
3 Plum Corner
Toytown
TO4 3ZH

Bobby Shaftoe
The Harbour
Toytown
TO1 1HH

Humpty Dumpty
The Wall
Toytown
TO4 3WW

Snow White
Dwarf Cottage
Toytown
TO3 2BT

Dumpty, Humpty, The Wall,
Toytown, TO4 3WW

Now try this!

- **Key the telephone directory into a chart on a computer.**

Work with a partner.

Teachers' note You could enlarge part of a telephone directory to read as a shared text. Use it to show the way in which it is organised. In the extension activity the children should key in the family name, personal name, address and telephone number in separate columns of a chart.

Developing Literacy
Text Level Year 3
© A & C Black

Sum it up!

- **Read the passages.**
- **Write a headline to summarise each of them.**

Use a dictionary.

---

1. 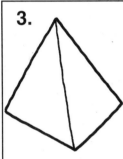 Dave Smith thinks there really is a monster living in Loch Ness. He has taken photographs of strange dark shapes in the Loch and, using heat sensors, has detected a huge living thing.

2.  Tea tree oil, an old Aboriginal medicine, is making a comeback. It has been used with great success to cure fungal infections like athlete's foot. Some doctors are now prescribing it.

3. 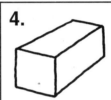 A Russian scientist has been researching pyramids. He has discovered a 'magic' about their shape. Force-fields have been measured around the six huge steel pyramids he has built.

4. A new trap which catches woodworms has been invented. Householders will no longer have to use poisonous sprays. A scent lures the insects into the trap, where they are caught by a sticky material.

Headlines

1. _____

2. _____

3. _____

4. _____

Teachers' note The children could work with partners, writing their headlines on scrap paper and re-drafting them until they are as brief as possible.

Developing Literacy
Text Level Year 3
© A & C Black